chasing euphoria

nicole mcallister

this book is for every young girl who was told
they were too opinionated-too passionate-too bossy,
for every soul who thought they were
not good enough for their dreams
or thought it was too late

i am eternally grateful for the love and support
i've received from my family
and my best friends,
delia, becca, alex, amanda, peter

heather duncan and jack bouley
inspired me with their friendship as well
as their belief in my poetry to write this book,
as they write books of their own

gus, roderick, claudia b-there aren't enough words
to describe the magic that occurs when you believe
in someone you don't know very well,
i'll always be thankful for your kindness

how painfully graceful
is a butterfly

alone they transform
patiently stuck,
curled up
for sometimes a week
or more
as they crawl out
of their cocoon alone
(their heart's core)
without much help
or they'll fall and die,
some caterpillars barely
make it out alive

after all,
the only way a caterpillar
will see the sun again
is as a butterfly

it takes courage
to save yourself

table of contents:

the golden hour

blind spots emerged
in the white sunshine
we became dizzy
from staring
into the light for

too long

that's how it felt
when we fell in love

i felt you
before i saw you
every single atom
inside me
picked up speed
and there was this

magnetic
          pull

as if the universe
was giving me
a gentle shove
towards you

your hand
outstretched
towards my heart

i didn't know it then
but you remembered us first

first impression

i can't tell
the ground
from the sky
when
you're around

i'm too busy
staring
into your eyes

with my head in the clouds

when you smiled
your soul kissed mine

it was like cinnamon
and wine to my
inflamed heart

anti-inflammatory

i am a terrible first date
you will feel
like you've known me
for an unexplainable
amount of time,
"no such thing as white lies" i'll say,
as i keep trailing on about
all my complicated ways

and you won't be sure
if you want a second date
but for some reason,
you asked me anyway

"it takes courage to
know yourself like that," you said
(i will always be grateful for that)

i forgot
how to smile;
you gave me
sage advice

and said,
"we'll keep
practicing"

you asked if it hurt
when i fell from the sky

to be honest,
i crawled out of the
earth's core

and it felt just fine

"do you
believe in auras?"
you asked me

pacing the corners,
smudging
the shadows
with sage

"yours is the color of
cinnamon," i said

making out until
five am
is better than sex

(with the right person)

your skin tastes
like sunshine

i think you
are light

my inner child
racing alongside yours
wearing cloud heels
in my kayak
wading through the
clouds like ships

i want you to be afraid
of how much you love me

my favorite
sunsets
are the ones

where you feel
the colors
more than
you see them

we wished
upon
the same star

that's how
i found you

stars typically
share the
places we hide

how pure of a love

the way the sky
embraces
the ground
with just
enough room
to be themselves

yet still together as one

i want
to create

cities on top
of clouds
with you

the earth keeps
saying
we won't last
that i should enjoy it
while i can

sticky sweet
like the way fruit
slowly ferments and
sunsets fade away

when we broke up
it was like a
sunburn on a cloudy day
i should have
known better
but i never saw it
coming

the sun
keeps dancing
in between
the clouds

can't make up
it's mind
until they're
long gone

i could have
lit sage in our home

but i kept threatening
to *burn* it

perhaps, i buried
your insecurities alive
and maybe
you did think i
deserved better
from wherever else

i know you dream
of me though,
because
i can't sleep at night

the best
type of revenge?

knowing
you will think
of me with
every sunset

some of
my darkest hours

were in
broad daylight

you called me
sunshine eyes

but now they leak
rainbows

raspy voice
of amber and maple syrup
that would sometimes
become a higher
pitch when excited
or intimidated

do you think about me?

will you someday
wish for those days again?

sun glitter
glowing in the
long grass
wishing i could
forget the way
you tucked
my hair back

(i look for you
everywhere)

star dust
that turned
into a
wallflower

you loved
that about me
once

i look for you in words
that were never yours,
underneath
feelings you never had

i wonder if you are missing
what could have been
as much as i am

red hot,
sticky sweet
you're never
going
to recognize me

you were
as predictable as
a sunset

i was more like
the northern lights

do you remember
the first time we met?

the moon
whistled at us
and i couldn't
stop blushing

drinking in
evening stock breezes
paired with
lavender clouds that could
take your breath away
with junebug symphonies
dancing inside my head

when you
let me fall asleep
on your shoulder
with such ease

these are the memories
i cling to;
this is what's left of us

beware of the tangerine leaves
who misinterpret
what you said
to back up what they
are saying as they
flip from one side to the next

when winds warn of a storm

i run lavender
through my hair
and wear it on my wrists

count the days
i don't wear daisy
as a measure
of your absence

knowing you'll never
recognize me
in this scent

i chase sunshine
on rainy days
to find the light

but you,

you tried to
steal the sun

you asked
for space

so i found
a new universe

in the darkness,
i hear silent tears fall

i dream of alien hotels
with saturnshine views
near tangerine moons

there are lollipops
and foggy windows

(there's still me and you)

i think about
my reaction a lot
you were a fire of passion
and i was a pot of
boiling water
i kept saying "baby it burns"
over things that couldn't
touch me these days

as time passes,
i gradually
grow into an ocean

enlightened

i'm miles away
and you're right,
it feels like
galaxies ago

you use to lay
beside
me on this hill
telling me how
we're both
universes

you dug me up
halfway

i can't tell if this is
what being planted
feels like or if you're
digging my grave

i thought
you were my moon
but i'm taking
back my gravity

you won't
be able to
manipulate my tide

i waited in the sunshine
so you wouldn't miss me

i kept a watchful eye out for you
glowing brighter impatiently,
i thought about all the things
we would do once you found me

you did and asked to bring
the darkness too-without a thought,
i said "yes, of course,
i accepted all of you"

but the darkness almost
consumed us both

i hide under a different sun
these days, embracing my shadow
as i patiently wait for yours
to find your way

if i ever see you again,
that amount of darkness
càn't come then

i never stopped
waiting
part of me thinks
i'll always
be waiting as though
my soul would
wait two thousand years
for five more minutes
with you

our love meant
that much to me

i'll be practicing
my smile, meanwhile,
just in case

sunspots burst
out of me

it hurts that
i hurt you

-why am i like this?

i miss the way we slept in
each other's arms-even when we
shared that futon couch
and the blanket kept slipping all night,
do you remember?
i miss your high pitch "ha" because i
always got you to laugh-i miss that,
i genuinely miss that

the long talks, the beach walks,
dancing in the car
(i'm sorry i told you i hated
your taste in music, i was lying
...we were in a bad spot then)

do you remember standing
on the couch? you took my hand at
the punk bar getting fucked up
spiritually on so many feelings;
i can't forget you

i sprayed your blanket with the
perfume you gave me after you told me
to move on like that would have made you
remember your love for me

i left the dried flowers too and the sign
you made me asking me out on a date,
i haven't regretted it yet because we could still
exist without those things i clung to...i knew i
loved you because i couldn't hate you, i tried

i hope you live a beautiful life,
i truly do, all i ever wanted was your
happiness-it looked so good on you
i wish we wore it out more
but i'll always be grateful for
the time i had with you

ashes to ashes, stardust to stardust
this is my white flag
waving at my living funeral;
these pieces of me had to die
in order for me to survive

i was persistent (just like you)
maybe if we're lucky
this next life, we'll get it right

i drink coffee
to calm down
these days

i look up dream meanings
of how i'm filled with regret
in frozen tears and sunsets;
i hear your voice dripping
amber everywhere

you're on my same
wavelength, though,
i can't interpret
what you are saying

i tried to
fill myself up

in empty
margarita glasses

(it only made these holes worse)

don't regret
shining
your light
so bright
onto
the darkest parts
of humanity

for that is where it
was needed the most

i welcome fear
right in and it
frightens
the one i love

facing my fears is
the sexiest thing
i could have done

i was your ride or die
but you left anyway

i ride for myself now
instead of be in love's daze;
once in a while,
i let gravity get on
but it's
usually just for
a song or two

and then it's me,
alone,
dancing in the universe
i created without you

i want to go
where the sun
is blue

with stars
so hot
the memory
of you melts and
my tears do too

we could have laid
to rest the broken pieces
of ourselves

you chose to
mock them instead;
used me as a tool
so i turned the
ground cold towards you

true love's flowers
would never blossom

some people
are so set
on seeing the
differences

that they'll
never see the
synchronicity

it went by so fast;

how unfair
and unfortunate

i almost forgot
to enjoy it

star-crossed lover,
i'll forever be missing you

love is the most
powerful of
connection

i think that's why
some of us break
and never pick up
the pieces
when it's over

everyone has
hurt someone
at some point
in time,
but our intention
behind it matters

(human nature)

you must fear yourself
to put fear into others

let it be

the way the grass
reflects anything but green

the way you promised
forever and then took it
away so suddenly

the way i haven't made
memories yet with
anyone else, including me

i promise myself
that i won't always
wait for you

change
is uncomfortable
for a short while

but staying is
misery forever

heartbreak
showed me
how much soul

i was actually
missing

you're wrong if you
think inspiration comes
from only happy thoughts
and pretty things

it wasn't until
my heart turned black
and the sludge that
dripped
down my chest
was the ink i used
to write to you

about the explosions
in the sky from the stars
who refused to accept
you're never coming back

get up

i know you
don't care right now
but one day you will

brush your hair,
floss your teeth,
take a shower too,
drink some water
with a couple deep
breaths after

(i promise,
you will feel better)

how can you not see
the magic that you are

the skies are painted
twice a day to show you

bold
was what
my courage
was
made of

civil twilight

after you left,
there was very
little love
and a hole in my chest

i took that hole
and dug deep
fingers scraping away
inside at the decay
of you and me
making room for
planted seeds of acorn,
dandelion and cinnamon trees

i only beg
the sun to stay now

imagining the sun
tracing the shadows
along my neck
as i hold my breath
trying to freeze time

i realize,

time has been
manipulating me

backs pushed
against the hill,
the place where i saw
the pieces last

you're on the other side
with your back arched,
head in your hands

i outstretch mine;
if i want forgiveness,
i have to learn
to forgive first

imagine the light
in the darkest of times

(how we paint the picture
is still in our control)

i let my jealousy
guide my ego,
i ruined a couple of sunsets
and some beautiful moments
instead of letting go

my intentions wanted
to love you
if only i had chosen
to stay mindful

blue moons are
for the lost wishes
forgotten by the stars

the moon is proof
that second chances
do exist

nicole mcallister

you could charm
monsters
with two heads,
your song moved
the dead and
summoned the rain

when you held her hand
electric currents
still ran through you

but you lost her anyway;
that's what happens
when you lose faith

i almost forgot
who i truly was

my dad reminded me
of all that i had done,
all the charitable work and
time i had put in;
he taught me that
a positive mindset in life
will always help someone

(thank you for always
being proud of me,
even when i couldn't be)

in broken pieces,
i find myself
searching at thinking spots
in the golden hour

picking up as many as i can
reflecting back at me,
i see the person i want to be

women are
the only
vessel that
delivers life

there is nothing
weak about that

we privatize water
and bottle up air

necessities as commodities
will kill humanity

a finite amount of resources

the greatest america
i can think of

teaches the history
of where the earliest
queens and kings
originated from

africa

love should never be hidden

there are invisible
people who deserve
to be seen

homeless

what strength it takes
to risk a better life,
to leave behind
the only world
i've ever known;
to knock on a door
i don't know

without guarantee
i will make it out alive
whether i stay or go

my future depends on if
someone answers me

refugee

i will
always stand

with
the dreamers

that's what america
is made of

i knew someone
who shared a smile
with everyone he saw...
i don't really know where
things went wrong;
i only wish i had
reached out more
when i wasn't sure
if his soul began
to feel sore

(check on your strong friends)

suicide awareness

we will
break
glass ceilings

illusions
will not cage us

rare
giraffes, rhinos,
leopards, tigers, elephants,
and gorillas
(just to name a few)

will be extinct
if we don't stop relentlessly
dominating nature
and change our world view

every plant-based choice counts
towards saving the planet

carbon footprint

healing is a process
that comes in waves;

tonight is a hurricane

in my darkest hour
friends made of plastic
preyed upon my sadness

do not hold these people
close out of fear
of being alone

they will take
and take and take
until you break

stop giving life
to your obsessions
that are
killing you

inner peace isn't
anywhere but
inside you

have you ever
loved someone
so infinitely
that you would want
their happiness
before your own?

in the darkness, alone,
as i was starving my ego
i found myself growing
in realization

how genuine
love could be;
for only the soul
knows how to do that

i put all my energy
into fear

then wondered why
i lacked courage

what we had was beautiful;
the kind of beauty
that explains why things
must end so experiences
can be truly appreciated

in order
for new beginnings
to break over the horizon

i still hear us laughing
every time i walk that path

i still feel the fireflies
lighting up our way

questioning our love
is like questioning
a sunset after it fades

energy imprints

what does falling
in love and
falling out of love
have in common?

both lose
track of time

befriend the cinnamon
flavored friends;

they don't sugar coat
a world that needs
to be saged

a gentleman is
exactly that

a gentle man

communicate
clearly with yourself

you will communicate
clearer with others

you taught me that i
am capable of love
in unpleasant situations

i taught you that
pleasant situations
need love too

your weirdness
is so
alluring
and
captivating

(it's truly entrancing)

if someone
calls you
complicated

it means that
strange
and powerful
are quite beautiful

i had spent
so much time
wondering why
you didn't
love me back

i keep wishing i had
given those
who actually did
a chance

i'm not sure if i knew
what love was then

there was a fork in the path,
i could walk through
the tangerine leaves brushed back,
a potential way
or i could walk through
the field of sage;
untouched and dying

i chose the latter,
blowing cinnamon kisses
everywhere that
needed it most

i witnessed a miracle
before the blue hour as fireflies
lit up that forgotten pathway

i rose sage back from the dead,
the cinnamon was manifesting;
looking down before i knew it,
i saw myself blooming

i gather up
the stars in the sky
and hide them where
my heart was
after you left

i wanted to be your
cinnamon girl
but i'll settle for
the stars instead

you are missing
from me
but
i am surviving

my gift is one
that only
the strong
can endure
for long;
empathy

transmuting
energy
both positively
and negatively
so carefully

neuroscience
inspired
me to challenge
my darkest
moments of
anxiety, fear,
and self-doubt

the more i knew
about my brain,
the more i could
communicate
what i needed
to be light

i wasn't proud of
the universe i created

so i manifested
a new one

self-awareness
gave me
the sight
that i create
my own reality

i didn't have to keep
breaking myself into
pieces to be better

you could have
pulled the clouds
a p a r t
like cotton candy

and

i still wouldn't have
been impressed

rearranging my priorities
with cinnamon on my mind
you saw me as an outcast
and then tried to exile me

i burn sage to set my tone

the outcasts
become the strongest queens
you will see
the power within as
tangerine leaves scatter
before me
as i tell the sun to not set
the day i take back my throne

for i am the dead risen again

and you could never control
those who ruled the
greatest empires alone

i stood by you
in your darkest hour

when the light
finally broke through
...you left

you took my love
for granted

i swore i would
never let someone in
ever again

i would take your
rejection a thousand
times over if it
meant i had to sacrifice
who i am now

you lost me
and i found myself

you picked apart
the colors of my
rainbow

so i explained how
i am worthy
of an
abundance of light

you empower others
when you
empower yourself

i'm convinced outside sources
conspired with the universe
over us out of jealousy

magic did exist and
electricity had reached
a whole new level of complexity;
our love beneath the trees
woke something inside me

i will forever be grateful
for you helped me
find my dream

your softness
is so beautiful

please don't let
heartbreak
take that from you

the blue hour

loneliness can play
tricks on you at first,
it may seem like
everything
you can't exist in

and then after a while,
it may seem like the only
way you can exist

i stopped
responding

i started
listening

codependency
nearly killed
my confidence

we hide behind people
when we don't want to
face ourselves

when you face yourself
your soul
becomes accountable,
self-sustainable,
and you depend on
no one

manifesting a
wholesome partnership

i eat sunshine with my dinner
and sunflower seeds in between

sometimes i drink dandelion tea
and other times
i stare at yellow things

color therapy gave me back
my confidence and my dreams

nicole mcallister

i stopped turning
sandcastles into homes

they stopped
slipping away

there are some
hearts who will
always be there for you

even when you
least expect them to be

an honest person
wonders how someone
can hurt
themselves with a lie

the liar
wonders the same thing
about the person
who can speak their truth

only one will give you peace

you
will be
the energy
you're
around
eventually

(choose carefully)

self-love is
listening to your soul;

nurturing that
little inner voice
despite
all the obstacles

it's not the addiction,
it's the lack of connection

it's the soul-crushing reality
of the world that
leaves you empty

some of us don't know
how to fill ourselves
back up

you can lie all you want,
can't lie to yourself

who are you trying
to convince?

i learn a lot
from the sun

it's shown me warmth
when no one else did

it showed up when
no one else would

and when it went away
it always came back again

thankful
for your existence

even if i no
longer exist
in your world

i daydream of
colors
that nobody
has ever seen

(keep secrets with yourself)

i don't blame you for
missing what you two had

you gave
so much of yourself
for so long

i would be missing pieces
of myself too

i want to be
as gentle as rain

for not even the
ice stood a chance

the most beautiful
thing i've ever seen
is the way my mother
transmutes my pain
into power

self-sacrificing
in the darkest moments
that only the strongest
love knows how to be;

when she kisses my forehead,
we rewind time because
i'll always be her baby

your mother's wedding day
was my heartbreak's anniversary;
a few days before cupid's arrow
could get a chance to mend this

asked me to leave you
in a little red store;
fire burning from my eyes
as i looked back (i regret that)

i think that day marked a month
of your sobriety of many things,
including all your lies

rewind six months of throwing up
from all the stress because i loved
you so much and chose to stay...
i'll always be grateful i did and
i'll always be grateful you let me go

(i almost missed out on my soulmate)

you told me
that you ruined lives

i didn't believe you
because you walked
into my life
and created sunshine

when you left
you inspired me to
create my own
instead
and i'll always
believe that

keep
your money;

i want to see
how wealthy
you really are

nicole mcallister

you can love
someone so loud

but if you don't
love yourself first
no one will ever
listen

clouds break apart

and piece themselves

back together still

the way you speak
to yourself

will set the tone
for how others
speak to you

passionate people
are rarely bored

for that,

i am eternally grateful
because the present
became a present

mindfulness

i embrace the truth
so i can put fate to the test

no lies, no fears
only letting the past rest;

how someone
loves you
is a reflection
of how they
love themselves

even on rainy days
the sun still rises;
let it be known,
i never needed you
it was only desire

i raise cinnamon clouds
from the ground
these days because
i am self-sustaining

i bring sage back
from the dead,
it takes less energy
to live this way

you thought i was falling,
but i was falling into place

if you have a bright light
it exposes the shadows
of everyone
everywhere you go
that is why it is important
to find others who
shine as bright

they are less
afraid of their own shadow

i drank blueberry cornflower tea
hoping you would communicate
with me but it never happened

our imagination
can break us

or save us

my best friends
cheer me on
with cinnamon
at sunset

they saw me
rising
when i thought
i was setting

keep your
plastic flowers
sprayed with
vanilla perfume

you can find me
in fields of lavender
with hints of
evening stock breezes

for everything dies
eventually,
but at least it was real

i remember you
in a way
that only the first
few seconds of
light breaking
through at sunrise
can describe it

even if you don't
feel the same
i embrace it,
i would rather feel
something

than nothing at all

the way the dark
folds
into the light,
exposing our truths
against our lies
is the strongest
thing to overcome

our shadow side
enhances the light in us

love is
the light
that guides
us
out of
the dark

nautical twilight

do you know what
the right path feels like?

the inner child in you
respects
the inner child in me;
peace and happiness
eventually
turns into harmony

never going to war again
for someone who
swears they love me

no more apologies
for speaking my mind

i don't care what you think;
my heart is aligned
and my soul is glowing

coming from a place
of soul so i attract
my soulmate

the more
i fill myself
with light,
the less room
there is
for darkness

a strong soul
stands bright
on their own,
a stronger soul
lights the path
for others to see

if you dance out
of the light
and into the darkness
even for a second or two,
you can always
dance back into the light

it's never too late

self-preservation
is attractive

*so is self-accountability
and commitment*

creating
gave me
the inner peace

i was
dying for

a heart like mine
was never meant
for war,
though,
i've been prepared
my whole life

if it's not simply
peaceful,
what's all the fighting for?

have courage;
fear barely knows
itself

if you want more peace,
be more peaceful

if you want more blessings,
be more of a blessing

the birth of something
new always
feels like death
at first;

the way
winter sacrifices
itself for spring

starving my ego
and reading new ways
to align
my mind, body, and soul

this time i'll be ready,
for i still believe in
a soulmate for
as long as i have a soul

fruits, veggies, ted talks,
walking among the trees,
family, good vibrations,
planting seeds
of flowers and dreams

overcoming sadness for me
meant going back
to my roots

do you think i was
giving back the love you
gave me when in the end
i was the only one
fighting for us?

is this what closure can be?

i try not to live
in the past

all the love we had,
i won't forget

but it no longer
encompasses my heart

you're looking for
a home in your lover
but your home is in you;
sage the corners of each room,
put sage on a spoon or in your
cinnamon tea, find solitude
to grow love again
if you ever want to feel free

looking towards the cosmos
gave me the sight to
stop looking back at you

with gratitude guiding my soul,
i am teaching myself
to be attracted to what
is good for my health

free will

if someone
doesn't believe in you,
chances are
they barely
believe in themselves

you may be
the only one
who does

and that is enough

listening to
this ache in my chest

i transmuted
my humiliation
into confidence

i took my self esteem
out of the hands
of others

i reflected on the parts
i liked most about myself

(you couldn't change
who i was becoming)

yoga has been a physical
release for my body

teaching my dna to let go of
unwanted memories
as downward dog aligns
my spine
and tree pose
grounds my soul

i wonder where all
the negative energy goes?
i imagine a giant black hole
is where i send mine to,
hoping it will transmute into
something entirely new

laughing
can
be so
aligning

(mind-body-soul)

when i look at
a couple in love

i wonder
how many times
did they
fall out of it
in order to find it

just like fireflies
dancing in between
the trees

i now see the light
has always
been inside me

i had to actually
believe it first

until i chose peace

i could have
never loved you

(the way you deserved)

the most sensual
form of
attraction for me

has always been
the way you
found my brain
to be my true beauty

nicole mcallister

is this what
courage feels like?

your hand
in mine

-vulnerable

you are a
thousand times
more
luminous
than you realize

nicole mcallister

nod your head
and tap your leg

swirl those lavender
shoulders to
your favorite beat,
who cares
if someone's
looking now

get up babe,
come dance
with me
as we dance
away our
broken heart's
memory

-turn up that song

tangerine skies
pierce through the
overgrown reeds

i stopped putting
others
before my needs
and it has made all
the difference

in a past life,
i must have
promised you
that i would
find a way...nothing
could separate us;
not even fear

our love will
guide us through
the darkness,
the stars swear it

we just haven't
remembered
our courage yet

soulmates

i promise to
love you
like a sunset;

where each new day
is a chance to
prove my love
for you
all over again

self-love

i thought i knew
everything then

i could have
told you
where the
rainbow ends

now i know
that i haven't
the slightest clue
of where the rainbow
even begins

i went
out on a limb
knowing it would
possibly break

but i had to
anyways

nothing else
cures a
soul ache

you are divine
purpose in itself,
with a
beautiful mind

please don't ever
downsize
your dreams

rose quartz healed
my broken heart,
sunshine thoughts
and opal rings
during yoga made
my tangerine leaves
less tart

if i never lost you,
would i have ever
found my art?

perspective

i would seek
the masculinity
inside me
for healing

i only ever found it
from a
feminine place

i've been chasing
an ache in
my chest

i haven't
regretted it
since

this book of mine
has saved me,
this book of yours
could save you

one day
it'll be printed
on hemp paper
inspired
by your life's purpose
of words needing to
come alive
to inspire someone else

for even a beetle
can be a firefly

i forgave
the person's
heart
i had
broken
the most

myself

euphoria is a state
of perception

some search
through sin
some search
through success

the only time i've
tasted it is when
i felt connection
from within

blue honeycomb eyes
gave me my sight back
blue dreams gave me the
voice that i had been missing

openness turned into wisdom,
truth became my heaven,
and i had finally found
the peace i was searching for

contentment

purple clouds
with bubblegum pink lining
in an aquamarine sky
inevitably transforming
into indigo clouds with
cinnamon lining
in a tangerine sky

-how time changes

you will feel like
the sunniest day
dreaming in fields
of lavender
watching the clouds
go by in the bluest of skies
along back roads made of dirt
as we talk about the universe while
picking locally grown, organic
strawberries and breathing in
evening stock breezes in-between
emitting enough light to create our
own sunshine whenever the sun
is too busy by loudly singing and
quietly running fingers through
cinnamon hair as we're
laughing so hard that
there's nothing but silence
as we slowly start
to finally dance

true love

there was he,
who saw me
as a sunset, only briefly

and then there was you,
who saw me
as the sun

when you reached
for my hand
i could finally see
the colors of our electricity

peace was
dripping everywhere

perhaps,
i could be too late
(but at last)
i reached back anyway

i won't be afraid to love again

nicole mcallister

how i control
my light
in the darkest
of times

is how i measure
myself now

sitting in the long grass with
honeysuckle winds
whirling by
watching the airplanes
in the cinnamon, rose sky
with lavender in my hair

you dreamt out loud
that we should chase
sunsets for a living;

"what a life without
any misgivings," i thought,
with your hand in mine

"how can you
believe in forever?"
they ask me,
"when even sunsets fade..."

"the sun also rises," i say smiling,
"though never the same way"

there are two things
i'm certain of;

love saves us and
forever does exist

Manufactured by Amazon.ca
Bolton, ON